T0198973

Where We Found Home

Written by Alyson L. DaCosta

Illustrated by Mandy Pettey

WestBow Press books may be ordered through booksellers or by contacting:

WestBow Press
A Division of Thomas Nelson & Zondervan
1663 Liberty Drive
Bloomington, IN 47403
www.westbowpress.com
1 (866) 928-1240

Interior Image Credit: Mandy Pettey

ISBN: 978-1-9736-7696-6 (sc)
ISBN: 978-1-9736-7697-3 (e)

Library of Congress Control Number: 2019915769

Print information available on the last page.

WestBow Press rev. date: 10/29/2019

WESTBOW
PRESS®
A DIVISION OF THOMAS NELSON
& ZONDERVAN

I would like to dedicate this book to the extraordinary and resilient children of In Step. My hope for them is that any child who has lived there—past, present, and future—will know they are seen, heard, valued, and deeply loved, and that they will have the foundation they need to live full and happy lives. This dedication also extends to the loving founders of In Step, Jeff and Carla Picicci, who live out a rare level of sacrifice in such a way that has resulted in saving hundreds of lives in the process. Their devotion and work ethic is uncommon, the result of which will surely be a long-lasting legacy. Lastly, this dedication is also for the caretakers, aunties, groundskeepers, teachers, volunteers, social workers, cooks, doctors, and the many, many others who have invested any amount of time into making this children's home such a special and life-giving place.

Have you ever heard of a country named Kenya? Kenya is a very beautiful place in Africa. It's a country that has big mountains and many different lakes. Along the coast, it has lovely beaches with white sand and blue water. It also has long, winding rivers where women come to wash their family's clothes, and animals like giraffes, lions, and leopards come to drink! And it has huge fields filled with nothing but tall, yellow grass and sprawling acacia trees.

These are some of the things that make Kenya a special place, but they are not the only things. See, in Kenya there are many children's homes as well. A children's home is where children go to live if they no longer have parents for some reason. And one day, many years ago, a couple from America decided to pack up their things and move to Kenya to open a very special home for children!

But when this couple first moved to Kenya, they could only buy a small brick house. And it only had a few small bedrooms—so where would they find the space to put children who needed a home? They thought about it and decided to wait until they could get a bigger place to open a children's home. But they really wanted to help people now!

They came up with an idea to help people find clean water, because this is something most Kenyan homes don't have. Actually, most homes don't have any running water at all! That means the women and children have to walk—sometimes very far distances every day—to find water.

They might have to walk to a lake, or a river, or find a pipe somewhere that brings the water up from the ground. Then they fill up their buckets and carry the very heavy water all the way back to their homes. But doesn't this sound like such a difficult way to get water?

Even though it's difficult, getting water every day is important because they depend on it for so much, just like you and I. They use it to wash their clothes and dishes in, they use it to take baths in, and they always keep some aside for drinking. But a lot of the time, the water isn't really safe to drink.

Sometimes it's dirty and could have things in it that make them sick. So, this couple tried to think of ways to get good drinking water to the people who needed it. And then one day they got a knock on their door...

When they opened it, a man was standing there holding a baby girl! He told them that someone had found her outside all alone, and she needed a home.

This baby was very special, and Baba and Mama, as they came to be called, knew they wanted to take care of her. They took her in and named her Mercy.

Not long after Mercy was brought to them, someone else came with another baby who needed a home. And then another baby was brought...and another and another! Baba and Mama never turned away any baby who didn't have a home.

Sometimes they would get a call from the hospital about a baby who had been left there. So, Baba and Mama would go get the baby and bring him home. Sometimes other babies were found left outside, just like Mercy, and someone would hear them crying and find them. Then they would bring them to Baba and Mama too.

One day, Baba and Mama's little home was bursting with too many babies! What were they going to do? They thought how nice it would be to own a piece of land that would be big enough to build a home on it for all the children to grow up in. And big enough to take in the new babies they knew would keep coming!

So, that's what Baba and Mama decided to do. They looked for a piece of land until they found just the right spot. The land they chose was very beautiful. In Kenya, many of the trees have large, bright-colored flowers on them. And in the places where it rains a lot, all the flowers and plants grow big and tall, and the grass turns a pretty, deep green color. There is an explosion of color everywhere—even the dirt has a red tint to it.

And at night when the sun sets, the sky turns all shades of pinks, yellows, oranges, and reds. It looks like a beautiful painting, except it's new each evening because it's always changing a little bit. It never gets tiring to watch. This beautiful land was the perfect place to build a children's home to remind them that they will always be loved and taken care of.

So, Baba and Mama bought this piece of land and started building their children's home! They built that great big dining room they needed and filled it with lots and lots of high chairs for all the babies. They built the schoolroom they had dreamed of having on their property so the older children who were starting to grow up would have a place to learn. And they hired their very own teachers to come to the property to teach the children!

The land Baba and Mama bought wasn't only big enough for all the buildings they needed—it also had a lot of extra, wide-open space. So, each day the younger children go on long walks along the red dirt paths with their caretakers, whom they call aunties. The aunties show them all the different types of flowers and trees there are. And they point out the different kinds of birds that are flying overhead or resting on the tree branches. The children call this their safari time, when they get to go exploring outside.

During this time, the older children are in school. They walk just a short distance from their house to the schoolhouse. Doesn't it sound nice to have such a short walk to school? It was important for Baba and Mama to have a school on their own property so the children could get an education. Can you imagine how difficult it would be to have to drive a couple hundred children to school every day because there are no buses?

After school, the children have time to play. They can swing on their swing set or they can run around and play soccer, which is very popular in Kenya. All over Kenya, there are always groups of children who gather after school to play soccer on the side of the road or anywhere there is a patch of grass or dirt big enough to run around on. But usually none of the children have a soccer ball to play with... so they make their own!

Children will find plastic bags, enough to make a big ball out of them, and then tie rope all around them to keep the bags together in the shape of a ball. And this is how most Kenyan children play soccer.

Sometimes they even play with bare feet, and they can still run fast and kick that ball hard! Thankfully, the children's home has soccer balls, but there never seems to be quite enough for all the children to play with!

But like any other family, the children don't spend all of their time just playing—they have chores to do as well. Sometimes they help with laundry, with cooking, and with gardening. There are many big gardens and even some greenhouses where a lot of their own food grows.

The gardens are filled with lettuce, watermelons, zucchini, squash, collard greens, beans, corn, and many other things! The children love walking through the rows of sprouting veggies and seeing all the things that are growing that they'll be able to eat at harvest time.

Every country or culture is known for some of the food they eat. For example, when people think of American food, they might think of macaroni and cheese, apple pie, or hamburgers.

And when people think of Italian food, they might think of pasta and pizza.

In Kenya, rice and beans or sukuma wiki (collard greens) and ugali (made from corn flour) are very popular foods. Both of these dishes are daily meals for most Kenyans. And these are some of the foods that grow in their gardens.

But can you guess what meal these children get most excited for? Spaghetti and meatballs!

Once a week, they have spaghetti night, and the children love it! This is a meal that Baba and Mama introduced to the children, because they had never had spaghetti before. Baba and Mama had no idea how much the kids would love it! The children get so excited when they know they'll be having spaghetti for dinner...and it's always a lot of work to clean up the messy dining room when they're finished eating!

After dinner and before bedtime, the aunties and older children clean up the dining room to get everything ready for the next day. They get buckets of water to wipe down all the tables and high chairs and to mop up the big dining room floor.

And do you know where they get all those buckets of water from? They get it from their own property because they have clean, running water!

Do you remember in the beginning of the story how Baba and Mama wanted to help people get clean water? Well, when they started building their children's home, as they were digging for wells, they found lots of water! It was like they had a river running right through their property underneath the ground.

They were able to get this water into their home and build showers, flushing toilets, and plenty of sinks with clean, running water! The land Baba and Mama chose had all the things they needed to take care of the children without them even realizing it.

So, really, Baba and Mama were able to get clean water to people who needed it...and they were able to open a children's home, too, just like they wanted. It only happened very differently than they had imagined. It all started with one little baby girl, one little brick house that was too small for a children's home, and one couple who kept on saying "yes" to any child who needed a home.

Printed in the United States
By Bookmasters